1st poetry reading at "Lions Mouth"
Sh. January 14, 2020

Becoming Trans-Parent, One Family's Journey of Gender Transition

poems by

Annette Langlois Grunseth

Finishing Line Press
Georgetown, Kentucky

Becoming Trans-Parent, One Family's Journey of Gender Transition

ACKNOWLEDGMENTS

This book would not have been possible without the love, knowledge, insight
and editorial expertise of my daughter, Anna, and her wife, Erica. Thank you
to poet confidante, Tori Grant Welhouse for her willingness to listen, read and
offer suggestions. I am deeply grateful to poet/teacher, Robin Chapman and the
writers group at Bjorklunden, where the missing poems were crafted, shared
and edited. I give thanks to Estella Lauter, Susan Moss, C.K. Kubasta and Jayne
Feldhausen who helped with constructive feedback. Thank you to my talented
designer, Michelle Rich, Schemedia, Inc.(Green Bay) for the cover design. I am
indebted to my husband John, son Andrew and daughter-in-law Karen who gave
their love, patience, perspective and encouragement. Finally, I am grateful to all
who have supported me during poetry readings at bookstores, cafes and churches
while sharing this personal journey through poetry

Disclaimer: Any references outside of our immediate family to actual people,
places or situations is a composite of events and does not represent actual
persons, living or dead, and is purely coincidental.

Publisher: Leah Maines

Editor: Christen Kincaid

Cover Art: Annette Langlois Grunseth

Author Photo: Matthew Koller, www.distinctionphoto.com

Cover Design: Michelle Rich, Schemedia, Inc., Green Bay, WI

Printed in the USA on acid-free paper.
Order online: www.finishinglinepress.com
also available on amazon.com

Author inquiries and mail orders:
Finishing Line Press
P. O. Box 1626
Georgetown, Kentucky 40324
U. S. A.

Table of Contents

*To my daughter
for having the courage
to be herself*

Change Is on the Wind

Becoming Trans-Parent

We were gathered in the family room
the day our son told us,
I've got an announcement that's a long time coming,
handing us a letter in an envelope.

The day our son told us
we read silently, he watched anxiously,
handing us a letter in an envelope.
I'm transgender, I identify as a woman.

We read silently, he watched anxiously.
Going forward I will finally live openly and fully as a woman.
I'm transgender, I identify as a woman.
We feel time-stopped shock, at the word woman.

Going forward I will finally live openly and fully as a woman.
After years of turmoil and questioning, I finally feel right.
We feel time-stopped shock, at the word woman.
I've begun to understand myself and discovered what makes me happy.

After years of turmoil and questioning, I finally feel right.
I've got an announcement that's a long time coming.
I've begun to understand myself and discovered what makes me happy.
We were gathered in the family room.

Change Is on the Wind

Milkweed

My thoughts try to catch up with your telling.
Already three months into hormone therapy?
Black eyed-Susans in bloom,
leaves starting to turn.

How did I miss this?
Your softer features,
smooth skin, a coy smile
changing like the season in front of me.

I watch milkweed
those dry pods splitting wide open,
birthing perfect rows of seed,
given away like a secret, one at a time,

each brown beginning broken free
on the shifting breeze,
with hair grown soft, so very soft.
Change is on the wind.

Naming My Grief

At your first cry the doctor decreed
It's a boy! Your gender was assigned.

We chose the name you will carry for life, Eric.
It was our gift to you.

Old Norse for "one ruler, ever in power".
Your middle name is after your father, John.

We cannot conceive the years you struggled,
the anxiety and discord you felt.

Becoming a woman, you decree a new name, Anna
derived from your mother-roots, Annette.

For your middle, you chose the girl name we picked but never used,
Kari, from your Norwegian great-grandmother.

We're touched by your thoughtful choices.
You are still "ever in power" growing into your new name,

yet the day you told us the court approved your female name,
I cried that night in bed.

At the Baby Shower

Couples were invited to the shower.
The guys were looking bored while
the women fussed over the cake,
decorations, and heaps of presents.

When the shower games started
the guys fled to a bar across the street
to drink beer, eat pizza, and watch football.
You, my son, stayed with the women.

I felt embarrassed for you, the only guy left behind,
I asked, *Are you sure you don't want to go with them?*
You said, I *want to be right here.*
I watched you finger party favors on the table,
later gushing over the gifts,
booties, bottles and layettes.

You ate your chicken salad,
bubbling along with the lady chatter.
The hosting friends knew.
I didn't, but noticed
your hair was longer on top
getting curly, like mine.

Avatars of Transition

I
Ambiguo
flashes on the screen
blinking again at login.
Why does this keep showing up?

Years later you told me
you were role playing with MUDs,
chatting live in IRCs,
creating an online persona,
you said it was
a pleasant escape from a difficult reality.

II
You burrowed deeper
into our blue couch,
wouldn't touch door knobs,
held your breath from pesticides settling on lawns,
stuffed towels under your door to keep out *bad air.*
You counted your steps back and forth
through the kitchen doorway.
You washed away discomfort until the shower ran cold,
scrubbed until your skin was hot,
escaped for hours at the computer,
Ambiguo pulsing on the screen.

III
When **AstroKari** popped up in email,
I wondered who that was. Then learned
you were gaming in a virtual galaxy
with a made-up college-girl persona,
AstroKari, avatar of hope.

No Regrets

When Dad was diagnosed with a fast growing cancer
                    you were quiet and didn't come to visit.

When he started inpatient chemo,
treatment poison flowing through an artery
into his heart, we wondered

                    were you scared too?

    Just before this news, you sprouted red-brown whiskers,
    and later told us everything felt wrong when you
    looked in the mirror and didn't know who was looking back.

The day you finally showed up at the hospital
the beard was gone. You looked different, happier,
but we still didn't know.

    Months later, you confessed that during Dad's treatment
    you drove two hours each way to come back home for electrolysis,
    plucked raw with shocks, too red-faced to show up
    at the hospital when you were in town.

You told us Dad's illness made you think
how life is too short and you didn't want to be 60 years old,
unhappy in life, still regretting.

Lost Seed

Ripe with autumn, milkweed pods
split by the wind, spill their seed to the future.
Walking in a white cloud, thoughts drift to my daughter.
She saved her sperm-seed, just in case.

I didn't want to rule out a family, she said,
her priceless treasure frozen somewhere in another city.
As hormone therapy began, estrogen made her sterile;
an empty word, like an echo from a hollow drum.

She bought time with safe-keeping.
A year later I asked, *Did you renew the contract?*
After months of discussion with her long-time wife
she said, *We decided—No.*

No storage. No more expense. No children.
For days I pictured a god in white lab coat
flushing away sperm, our beloved bloodline.
These autumn days blur, a shroud of 'never' hangs on.

Cryogenics was preserving hope forever, or as maybe.
I never thought I'd cry over abandoned sperm.
Walking in white wind on this short autumn day,
a disappearing sun steals light from the empty pod in my hand.

The Child I Carried

The Child I Carried

Kicks and turns danced in my belly
I felt certain of a daughter.
Dad and I sang lullabies through my stretched skin,
saw a foot crease along the equator of this miraculous globe.

Waiting, waiting, until that day,
when I labored and pushed you into waiting hands,
thrilled, yet surprised, to hear the doctor say,
You have a son.

You grew up a sensitive soul, asking philosophical questions.
As a teen you chose computers, math, science and sitting with the girls.
The boys teased you for giggling,
yet to us, you seemed more geek than girl.

Your womanhood stunned us,
but when I told you
I thought I had carried a girl
you looked like I had just given you the moon.

The First Time I Enter a Ladies Restroom with My Daughter

When you were three years old, I knocked on the men's room door,
and taking your hand, opened the door cautiously.

I'd never been in a men's room before.
Urinal against the wall, a small white cake

of air freshener down in the porcelain,
only one stall with a door,

stainless steel, no pink wallpaper,
no silk flowers in a vase on the vanity.

I felt awkward, while you felt proud to go on your own,
still needing help right there in the men's room.

Thirty years later, you have transitioned into a beautiful woman
with long curly hair touching your shoulders,

a hint of blush on high cheek bones, pink lips,
a necklace of crystal beads resting on your collarbones.

After lunch you don't think twice when we head to the ladies room.
I wonder—do you feel tentative like I did long ago in the men's room?

But you look like you know where you are going.
I scan the room to see if other women are looking at you, at us.

Surely, someone will notice. But they don't.
Ladies keep fixing their hair, check their teeth for lipstick,

fumble for lip gloss in their purses.
We wash and dry our hands, fluff our hair,

you tuck in your blouse, we reach for the door,
I re-enter the world with my daughter.

The Child I Carried

Sharing Clothes with My New Daughter

She needs clothes.
Her budget is tight, my clothes are tighter.
I start in the middle of the closet
pull out the green sweater,
slacks in blue, black and brown,
two pairs of boot-cut jeans, skirts,
and a black dress I wore to a Christmas party.

The pants and tops fit her (we're both tall).
She rejects my middle-aged skirts
as any fussy going-through-puberty teen
who just started hormone therapy might do.
She scrutinizes my career suits, silk blouse
and navy pant suit laid across the bed,
finally choosing jeans and V-neck tops.

Next, our heads bend over my jewelry box,
fingering pierced earrings and beaded necklaces.
She picks up my grandmother's cameo,
the one I wore to prom decades ago.
She holds the ivory silhouette to her throat,
and with a soft brush of her hand
pushes her long curls out of the way.

At the Clinic

> *Many transgender people take hormones to transition to their*
> *identified gender. Some undergo gender-affirming surgeries,*
> *but many cannot access this kind of healthcare, and others live*
> *happily without pursuing surgery at all. There is no one 'right' way to*
> *transition.* —Anna

The cough is worse
she's three hours away from her
specialist in transgender health.
This cold has gone hard into the chest.

For anyone else
a trip to the family doctor would be routine.
But in a small-talk town,
where people give second looks, she worries.

She sits on a crinkly exam table,
paper ripping as she shifts from one thigh to the other.
Rubber soles come squeaking down the hall.
The door opens, she's wrapped in a paper drape.

> *(Footnote: Doctors/nurses take note: If what's under the sheet*
> *doesn't match what's in your mind, remain calm. Do your work*
> *with the same love and care as you do for everyone else. Many do*
> *not seek care because they fear that gasp, that judging look.)*

The doctor listens to her chest, *Bronchitis,* he says.
She gets a script for an antibiotic
from the doctor who advises her,
Eat some yogurt to prevent a yeast infection.

Not an issue, she snickers under her breath.
Next time, don't be surprised if I ask
about a mammogram and a prostate exam
in the same appointment.

In the Neighborhood

Middle School kids on the street follow her home.
They shout, *Hey! Are you a man or a woman?*
She crosses to the other side of the street,
keeps walking, ignores their words, keeps walking.
More shouts, *Hey! Hey! Are you a man or a woman—*
until she reaches her apartment,
opens the door, locks herself inside
to make dinner for her wife.

Shopping for clothes the sales person asks,
Can I help you, miss?
She beams, *Does this scarf go with this blouse?*
A man walks past, he looks, and looks again,
his eyes go up, then down, he keeps walking.
He sizes up women, he notes she's tall,
she's tall, for a girl.

After a Long Talk with My Daughter

On my walk I see a mallard mother
lead her string of ducklings to water.
I watch her charges slip into the pond as
she touches each tiny beak,
all accounted for, each yellow fluff.

As your mother I can't fix what others think.
I can't help you have all good days.
I can no more keep you safe in bathrooms,
hire you, or make you love yourself every day
than this mother duck can keep her offspring away from
that Muskie lurking below the surface, ready to pull one under.

But we both try.

If only I read more, talked to more "parents of"
or crafted better arguments to convince doubters.
Today I watch mother mallard and her string of ducklings
paddle away, knowing she cares for them as best she can
until it's their time to fly.

Instinctively, I know we're both doing our best,
our very best.

The Child I Carried

How Are the Boys Doing?

Friends I haven't seen in a while ask,
How are the boys doing?

Uh, my kids are fine. Yes, they are fine.
Both children are out on their own, married, doing well.

I use every gender neutral term I can
while weighing the situation:
> How much time do you have?
> How public is this place?
> How will my friends handle what I'm about to say?

"The boys" are now a daughter and a son.
Our son became a daughter.

My friends stare with silence.
I am certain it will be either
a long conversation
or a short one.

Younger Brother Speaks

We grew up playing with Legos and Micro Machines,
spent hours roller blading with street hockey.
We went on the same family road trips,
inching our hands over the imaginary middle line of the back seat.
We camped out, hunted bugs and fossils, skipped rocks across a lake,
hiked trails in the woods, panned for gold, played Huck Finn on a river,
found a gigantic toad in a tree stump to scare our mother.
No matter what, our shared experiences still happened.
Brother or sister, you're still the same person.

The Child I Carried

Tears of Joy

Giddy about a grandson, my parents rushed to the hospital.
As I was wheeled to a room, my Dad appeared in the hallway,

gave me a hug, two big tears rolling down his cheeks.
It was the first time I saw him cry; his little girl with a grandson.

Our boys loved their playful Poppa, wishbones hidden in his pockets,
handmade storybooks appearing in the mailbox to their delight.

He taught our boys to fish at Duncan's pond, ski at Sylvan Hill,
play backgammon at the kitchen table.

Wish you were here now, Poppa, I know you'd still
weep tears of joy for a grand-daughter.

Social Justice

How is it Love

You say you still love her, but *from a distance.*
When you quote scripture telling me *your* God is telling you
my transgender child is possessed by a demon and is perverted,
I reply: *No one has sinned here.*

You say, she is welcome, *only if she intends to change her mind.*
I say, *her mind has always been female.*
Aren't we all made in the image of a creator,
each one different, perfect and loved?

You tell me you cannot use female pronouns or the new name.
You say you still love her, but she is not allowed to stay in your house.
I ask..... *What if it was your child transitioning, born of your own flesh?*
You say..... *I don't want to talk about it anymore.*

You say you still love her, but *from a distance.*
How is it love when you practice
Love thy neighbor, except for those folks over there.

Gender Dysphoria
*gen·der dys·pho·ri·a – When a person's internal sense of
gender doesn't match the sex assigned to them at birth.*

Opposite of euphoria,
dysphoria is anxiety that grows
    undefined at first
        like being in a dark woods
            lost or something, but worse
often perched at the edge of an abyss

        not aware of what is possible
    still not fitting in
        with the jocks, or the preps,
            a guy, but not a guy.

Something feels definitely wrong,
    a disconnection from others' expectations
        more than not conforming,
        like being in a parallel universe

some people say, *it's just a phase*
            or, *why can't you just be gay*
and that makes her feel even worse.

Dysphoria hangs on day and night,
        where her nights are wakeful and days demand sleep.

Fact is, the true sense of self is real (euphoric)
Fact is, transition is difficult, she can't choose how others will react
        (many are rejected by their families)
Fact is, 40 percent of transgender people lose hope; attempt to end
their lives

unless

they get love (the unconditional kind)
      loved for being who they are
and accepted (the fit-in kind)
      where we help them feel worthwhile, valuable.

Truth is, for those who see no love or inclusion,
      their journey often ends, badly.

Our family rejoices, she's found her way
and yes, she's still with us.

Social Justice

Halloween Fright

(After The Frat Boys by Leslea Newman
from October Mourning: A Song for Matthew Shepard)

A male friend says,
Hey, wouldn't it be funny
to dress up like that athlete who became Caitlin?
Hey, wouldn't it be a riot
if I put on a long brown wig over my short hair
and wore a tight white dress and heels?

Hey, wouldn't it be hysterical to parade around
for Trick or Treat, making fun of a transgender woman?
You know, it's Pop Culture. Harmless fun.
Hey, I thought you could take a joke.

I'm not making fun of your daughter.
It was all in fun.
I'm offended that you're offended.

Justice for All
*48% of surveyed employers preferred a less-qualified
applicant over a more-qualified transgender applicant.*
—*Office of Human Rights*

On Sunday the righteous pray
to serve, to help others.

On Monday with prayer fresh on your tongues,
will you include my transgender daughter?

She's someone. Will you let her tell you about her skills?
She's has two college degrees,

can write algorithms, program and install computers,
design solar energy systems—all math and science smart.

She'll stay late; figure it out, be part of your team.
She patiently helps and teaches others.

She's terrified of being rejected.
Many like her are shunned, live in poverty,

are denied medical care and the right to earn a living.
She didn't choose this path, it chose her.

Today, when she comes knocking
will <u>you</u> choose her?

Social Justice

Health Risks for a Transgender Woman

She fears what the doctor might say about who she is and worries about discrimination or disrespect by medical providers. Will necessary medical appointments, lab tests and prescriptions be covered by health insurance? What will happen as she ages; what are the long-term effects of taking these prescriptions? What if she can't pay her medical bills? Will she live in poverty? What if she can't afford the doctor and decides to administer hormones without regular check-ups and critical monitoring? What if she gets so depressed she turns to alcohol and other drugs to cope? Will she ever be able to afford gender affirming surgery if she chooses to have it? What if she doesn't have thousands and thousands of dollars to transition, just to live? What if other people don't understand? What happens if she doesn't feel safe? What happens if people bully her or ignore her human rights?

Pronouns, It's Personal

*prō͵noun/ takes the place of a noun referring to the
participants in a discourse. He and she are gender-specific
third-person, personal pronouns. A gender-neutral pronoun
is not associated with a particular gender. The English
pronoun they is a gender-neutral third-person pronoun
that can refer to any gender.*

No need to be
bound to binary
coded as he or she,
one or the other
like computers,
programmed in 1s or 0s.
Some folks are neither (or neutral)
"they, their or theirs,"
singular and plural.
(English teachers, get used to it.)
There is also non-gendered
"hir" and sometimes "ze"
taking their place in diversity.
If it sounds queer,
funny to your ear,
know that you will
get there with "their".

Social Justice

Trans Etiquette

Questions people ask about my daughter:

Which bathroom does she use?
Did she have *the surgery?*
Does she have a penis?
How do they have sex?
Are you sure she isn't just gay?
Why doesn't she look more like a woman?
Does this make her a lesbian?
Does she like guys now?
What's her *real* name?

How I answer these questions:

Which bathroom do you use?
What *surgery* have you had?
Do you have a penis?
How do you have sex?
Are you sure you aren't just gay?
Why don't you look more like a woman?
Are you a lesbian?
Do you like guys now?
What's your *real* name?

I'm the Daughter You Always Wanted

Embracing Your Name

At first I took it personally
when you changed the
masculine name we gave you.
But as you've grown feminine
you wear your new name like a fine jewel.

Saying your name felt awkward at first
like writing a signature with the wrong hand.
But now your name rolls off my tongue easily
and the old name, while a fond memory,
feels odd to say.

In the midst of change you are still my child,
only now, you flow like a well-penned signature.

I'm the Daughter You Always Wanted

Wings

Black and yellow stripes inch along milkweed
then spin into a chrysalis that dangles
like a green gem until it transitions
into a butterfly with strong wings that can fly
very, very far.

Our daughter did that too.
You may not understand her biology,
but like the Monarch, she transformed,
has acquired wings to be herself,
the best cloud catcher I know.

Love and Marriage

From the beginning
they were soulmates.
He and She.

They married
and loved as one.
His and Hers.

They finished each other's sentences
thought the same thoughts,
loved the same things.

Even their family doctor found them both
so alike he asked in jest
if they were the same person.

After all these years they still stare
like newlyweds into each other's eyes,
but now the towels are embroidered
Hers and Hers.

I'm the Daughter You Always Wanted

Facebook Says We've Been Friends for Three Years

Yes, it has been three years since you told us; then changed
your name, grew your hair long, and started hormone therapy.
You changed your driver's license, passport, email address, and
set up a new Facebook account.
And today, we have a "Friendversary" of three years.
But of course we've been acquainted since conception,
you growing within, then around me, for three and a half decades.

One hot day last summer you tucked braids
close to the crown of your head.
Hair pushed back, I caught a glimpse of the past;
your broad nose, firm brow, the well-known forehead freckle
that is almost always covered with curls.
I feel like any mother who sees what was and is
as her child becomes an adult.

Three years ago you started over as a woman,
in that time, Facebook says we've exchanged 653 "Likes".
And in three years I've learned, my beautiful child, that life goes on.
Life just goes on; and I "Like" that.

Key Change

Live as if you were living already for the second time
—Viktor Frankl

She sings her own song
a contemporary score
composed in new ways
perhaps dissonant to some
but not to those who really listen.
It's still beautiful music.
Well-measured
it comes from the same place
but arranged in a new tune.
The melody exudes happiness
the harmony is real.
You can't fault the composer for that.
Remember Stravinsky's Rite of Spring
shook people up in their time.
Listen as she brings you into the light
with her song, a symphony even.

I'm the Daughter You Always Wanted

When Your Child Comes Out

I often think of the day you were born when
I held my sweet boy for the first time,
marveling *where did you come from?*
It's a lot to take in, when your child comes out.

As I go upstairs to bed I stare at old photos in the hall,
your short-cropped hair, striped shirt, toddler jeans,
that little-boy smile. I walk past you in a suit and tie for
graduation. At Christmas tears still well up as
my fingers trace the "old" name on the stocking.
It's a lot to take in, when your child comes out.

But now you walk with confidence,
meet new people with ease,
get together with women friends.
Your skin is soft like pink on a peach,
your blue eyes sparkle, your child-like humor has returned
and your familiar expressions are back.
You are the same person
only now that doubting discord is gone.
You live through yourself, instead of beside yourself.

You are the daughter I always wanted.

Epilogue
Way Finding

Who decides gender? Is it the attending doctor, midwife or person who assists at the birth? Or is it the person who knows who they are? For some, gender identity is quickly known, for others it can vacillate between times of doubting coupled with assurance. Gender is a spectrum that transcends stereotypes; it's a continuum of identity. It is my hope this collection of poems breaks through old stereotypes to open peoples' minds to what is possible.

Our daughter is an adult, our parenting is done but our worry, support and unconditional love continue always. As we go about our days we hardly talk about it anymore; yet the work has just begun. Gender identity is the continuing march for equality, the struggle for basic human rights: Bathrooms, equal employment, fair housing; available, affordable healthcare, legal marriage, and overall acceptance. She is finding her way, now we must support others so they can find theirs.

Transgender Resources:

Family and Ally Support: www.pflag.org

Medical Guidelines: www.wpath.org

Advocacy and Information: www.forge-forward.org

Large scale research survey - Transgender population in the US: www.ustranssurvey.org

National Center for Transgender Equality: www.transequality.org

Notes on poems:

"Becoming Trans-Parent" is a pantoum. This poem form has a set pattern within the poem of repetitive lines. The pattern in each stanza is where the second and fourth lines of each verse are repeated as the first and third of the next. The first and last lines are the same.

"Avatars of Transition", references are made to 1990s computer technology:
MUDs are *multi-user dungeons*, an early type of online computer game that used text only.
IRCs refer to *internet relay chat*, the early version of chat rooms or list servs.

"Gender Dysphoria"
•The definition of gender dysphoria used in the epigram is the one used and preferred by transgender people: "*When a person's internal sense of gender doesn't match the sex assigned to them at birth.*"
•The attempted suicide rate of 40 %, source: page 9, 2015 US Transgender Survey www.ustranssurvey.org . "Among the starkest findings is that 40% of respondents have attempted suicide in their lifetime—nearly nine times the attempted suicide rate in the U.S. population (4.6%)."

Annette Langlois Grunseth has a BA in Radio-TV-Film/ Communications from the University of Wisconsin-Madison and is a lifetime member of the Wisconsin Fellowship of Poets. Her poems have appeared in *Wisconsin Academy Review, Midwest Prairie Review, SOUNDINGS: Door County in Poetry, The Poetry Box's/Poeming Pigeons, The Ariel Anthology* and other publications. Several of her nature poems were set to original music and performed at Acadia University in Nova Scotia. She is retired from a career in Marketing and Public Relations and lives in Green Bay, Wisconsin, with her husband, where they both advocate for equal rights.

After the surprise of learning about their oldest child's transition, Annette and her husband, John, offered immediate and unconditional love which has taken their family on a journey of understanding, empathy and acceptance. Annette shares her poetry as a way to increase awareness, one audience at a time. To know someone firsthand dealing with gender transition is to dispel myths and stereotypes about gender identity. John, a retired human resources professional, stays on top of employment, healthcare and human rights law. Together they tackle the issues essential to their daughter and other LBGTQIA citizens. Annette is also an avid outdoors woman who enjoys kayaking, bicycling, camping and exploring our national parks.

Contact:
www.annettegrunseth.com

CPSIA information can be obtained
at www.ICGtesting.com
Printed in the USA
LVOW08s0324030617
536790LV00004B/5/P